CONTENTS

PRACTICAL
BREAKTHROUGH
PRAYER
DECLARATIONS
&CONFESSIONS

THE WORD IN YOUR MOUTH

CHRIS GBENLE

CGB
PUBLISHING
SCOTLAND

Practical Breakthrough Prayer Declarations and Confessions

Chris Gbenle

Published by CGB Publishing Scotland

Text copyright © Chris Gbenle, 2020

First published 2020

ISBN 978-1-9996053-2-2

Cover design/layout: Imaginovation Ltd.

Printed in the United Kingdom

DEDICATION

This book is dedicated to the Holy Spirit who prays in and through us.

APPRECIATION

My special gratitude goes to the Most High God, the lover of my soul whom I graciously encountered in a powerful way more than three decades ago. Thank you my dear Lord for taking good care of me and for counting me worthy to be a vessel in Your hand.

I thank all members and friends of the Fountain of Love Parish of the Redeemed Christian Church of God, Aberdeen, Scotland who most lovingly encouraged me by taking these prayer declarations seriously and thereby obtained good reports as they used the confessions in faith.

To my dear wife, Nike Gbenle, a co-labourer in prayer with me, my best friend and life companion, I say thank you. Your encouragement (more like insistence) that we put these prayers together is most appreciated. Love you loads.

My thanks go to our children (Demi & Cyril, Dami and Dara) who the Lord has most graciously granted us the privilege to raise for His glory. Though we prayed a lot for you, but you never became prayer points. Thank you for your obedience and love for your parents.

Special thanks to my Senior Pastor and Mentor, Kola Bamigbade who gave me the platform in the Region to develop my prayer ministry. I am eternally grateful to you and your wife, sir.

Without any shadow of doubt, I am what I am by the grace of God. Father, you have been my great Helper and coach all the way. Thank you for picking me up and raising me from the dust. I owe you everything Father. To you alone be the glory now and forever. Amen.

I will like to appreciate the hard work of the group of friends headed by a dear fellow minister Stanley Okosodo, who helped with the publication of this and other books.

I pray you will not lose your rewards in Jesus' name.

INTRODUCTION

From the early days of Church history, confession of belief has always been a central part of our precious faith. Various convocations and councils were called through the centuries to look into what the bona fide follower of Jesus Christ should believe and hold on to as the ground and basis of their belief.

These early fathers of our faith based their call to clear confession of faith on the word of our Lord Himself - *For by your words you will be justified, and by your words you will be condemned.* Matthew 12: 37. The Lord also told us that - *"For assuredly, I say to you, whoever says to this mountain, 'Be removed and be cast into the sea,' and does not doubt in his heart, but believes that those things he says will be done, he will have whatever he says."* Mark 11: 23. The Lord placed a lot of emphasis on what a person says as much as what the person does.

Our words are the threads we use to weave the tapestry called our lives. The quality and attractiveness of the tapestry can be traced back to the threads used to weave them. While the words we use in our daily activities are important, the words we use in prayers are much more important. Words are powerful and prayer is said to be the greatest force on earth.

While there are prayers of petition and supplication in which we plead with the Lord to intervene in situations and circumstances; there are also prayers of bold confessions and declarations. Many prophets of old put their convictions into prayers in a bold confessional manner, and the Lord honoured their words.

David spoke boldly of what he expected the Lord to do when he was about to face Goliath as recorded in 1 Samuel 17: 46 – 47. *"This day the LORD will deliver you into my hand, and I will strike you and take your head from you. And this day I will give the carcasses of the camp of the Philistines to the birds of the air and the wild beasts of the earth, that all the earth may know that there is a God in Israel. Then all this assembly shall know that the LORD does not save with sword and spear; for the battle is the LORD's, and He will give you into our hands."*

Was the above pronouncement by David a prayer or a threat to Goliath? David in the quoted passage of scripture was speaking first to the hearing of God. When we pray, we speak so that the Lord may hear us and act accordingly in our favour. God has even promised that when we speak and God hears, some actions follow from His side. *Say to them, "As I live," says the LORD, "just as you have spoken in My hearing, so I will do to you."* Numbers 14: 28. That is why it is better to load you prayers with positive words. Don't go before God and complain and drag yourself down. Speak words that speak of hope and victory and God will do as you say unto His hearing.

Second, David spoke to the hearing of people standing around, including David himself. There are times that it is wise to pray aloud. Someone's faith might be challenged and encouraged by you doing so.

Finally, David spoke so that the enemies of God may hear. The visible and invisible enemies of God need to hear what God is doing or has purposed to do for you, so that they may fear the only Mighty and Living God.

The purpose of these prayers is to speak them out (confess) as much as it is possible. There is power in our confession. *For by your words you will be justified, and by your words you will be condemned.* Matthew 12: 37. There is much power in prayerful confessions and confessions of prayers.

Elijah was presented to us as the classic man of prayer who we are expected to follow. *Elijah was a man with a nature like ours, and he prayed earnestly that it would not rain; and it did not rain on the land for three years and six months. And he prayed again, and the heaven gave rain, and the earth produced its fruit.* James 5: 17 – 18. But looking closely at Elijah's prayers, He made many powerful declarations in the course of his 'fire' ministry. He stayed long at his prayer altar when he needed to, yet many examples of Elijah's kind of prayer recorded for us were declarative prayers.

The prayer that shut the heavens referred to in James 5: 17, was a simple - *"As the LORD God of Israel lives, before whom I stand, there shall not be dew nor rain these years, except at my word."* 1 Kings 1: 17. That was all we were told Elijah said.

A New Testament Christian may have prayed the same prayer in contemporary English like this – "Because I am a child of God, filled with His Spirit, I declare that no rain will fall henceforth, not even a drop in Jesus' name. Amen."

As it worked for Elijah, I am confident it will work for you as long as you are a child of God. We are also aware that when it was time to bring down the rain again, Elijah had to intercede for a reasonable length of time, and not just a simple command. There is much to say about that – The mercy of God must be carefully and persistently sought. It is not just on demand; it is the prerogative of God and He shows it unto whom He wills.

The point must however be made that confessional and declarative prayers are bona fide means of addressing heaven when there is a need and the earth cannot but respond.

The Lord Jesus Christ encouraged us to pursue such approach in our prayers when He said in the Gospel according to Mark, chapter eleven and verse twenty three: "For assuredly, I say to you, whoever says to this mountain, *'Be removed and be cast into the sea,' and does not doubt in his heart, but believes that those things he says will be done, he will have whatever he says.*".

For the various situations and circumstances of our lives, there are words based on the living word of God available to counteract negative happenings and enforce good things.

The passage of scripture quoted from Mark's gospel above laid a singular but important condition for declarative prayers to work. You must believe what you are saying. And if you do, it will of a truth work for you. May the LORD answer you in the day of trouble; *May the name of the God of Jacob defend you; May He send you help from the sanctuary, And strengthen you out of Zion.* Psalm 20: 1 – 2.

CHAPTER ONE

THE EXPECTED OUTCOMES OF THE RIGHT USE OF THIS BOOK

A tool is as good as the person who uses it and a weapon will only do as much damage according to the dexterity and the power that the holder of the weapon possesses.

For every tool, some instruction manual must come with it and sometimes it may be necessary to show the person who will use it the rudiments of the techniques of use. It is likewise important to know the potential of the resource at hand.

1. *There will be a release from fear of the situation you may be facing.* The most potent weapon in the hand of the enemy is the spirit of fear. It paralyses, and it can turn a winning situation into an epic loss. Your confession drives away fear and draws in faith. The young lad David who killed

the Philistinian Goliath was not immune to fear when he faced the man-mountain. He admitted to his disposition to fear when he said in his Psalm – *"My enemies would hound me all day, for there are many who fight against me, O Most High. Whenever I am afraid, I will trust in You."* (Psalms 56:2-3) But in the face of fear, David made his declaration loud and clear for all to hear. When you do the same, fear shall disappear, and victory shall appear in all its glory in Jesus' name.

2. **There will be an increasing level of boldness spreading through all areas of your life.** A person incapacitated in one area is likely to feel weakness spreading to other areas as well. It works the same way for strength. It is a spiritual principle that has worked through the ages. *They go from strength to strength; Each one appears before God in Zion. Psalm 84: 7.* As you take these declarative prayers in your mouth and into the presence of God, the automatic outcome is a progressive increase in strength and confidence in the Lord.

3. **You will be an influencer of people for God.** Your testimony is your most priced asset, keep it well. The people around you will soon discover that your words are not fearful or negative anymore. When they see miracles following you,

2

they will be convinced that your God is indeed a miracle Worker who does great things for those who declare Him boldly.

4. **You will grow in the knowledge of God and the ability to pray.** One of the things you will discover as you use this book conscientiously and correctly is that the ability to craft your own prayers will be developed and grow in leaps and bounds. More than anything else, prayer draws us closer to God. It is impossible to pray well and long and still not know God well and deep. Yes, God will answer your prayers and resolve all problems as you take these words into your mouth, but He will do more than that; the Father will show you His ways and draw you close to Him. The word of the Lord to His people in the book of Second Chronicles, chapter seven and verse fourteen says: *"If My people who are called by My name will humble themselves, and pray and seek My face, and turn from their wicked ways, then I will hear from heaven, and will forgive their sin and heal their land."* Prayer is all about seeking God's face, and not just about looking up to Him for handouts. The workings of the Kingdom of God is that God draws close to us when we draw close to him, as James wrote in the book of James chapter four, verse eight. Based on the eternal truth of the word of God, I can guarantee that your relationship with

3

God will never remain the same as you use these declarative prayers.

5. *You will produce spiritual fruits in abundance.* The surest objective evidence of our relationship is the fruits we produce. As important and necessary as it is to see great signs and wonders, it is the fruits we bear that is the *sine qua non* of our faith. The Lord Jesus Christ put it this way – *Therefore by their fruits you will know them.*
Not everyone who says to Me, Lord, Lord, shall enter the kingdom of heaven, but he who does the will of My Father in heaven.
Many will say to Me in that day, Lord, Lord, have we not prophesied in Your name, cast out demons in Your name, and done many wonders in Your name?
And then I will declare to them, I never knew you; depart from Me, you who practice lawlessness! Matthew 7: 20 -23.

Prayer changes us more than it changes things. That is why the end of prayer is not necessarily the precise answer to your request at the very first mention. We learn patience through prayer. The more we pray and we have to wait for the answer, the more we recognise the important work the act of praying is doing in our lives. Humility is another virtue we learn and grow in as we pray. Self-sufficient people do not see any need for prayer. And yet, God expects us to depend on Him as our source all the time. These prayers as you say them and turn them into your own words will impact you and make you more like the person Jesus wants you to be.

CHAPTER TWO

HOW TO USE THE PRAYER MANUAL

This suggested approach to the use of this prayer manual is only a guide. It is expected that you will work with what works best for you. For those who have not used a similar compilation before, the method suggested here will serve as a quick start instruction and as you learn the rope, you will be able to operate with more freedom.

1. Choose one of two ways in which you can use these declarative prayers. Do you want to use it as a 'sit-down' menu in which you set aside adequate time in preferably a quiet location? Or, do you want to use it 'on-the-go', in which you pick one or two points and you use them as you carry on with your daily activities? I will suggest you use both methods depending on the time you have.

2. If you have decided that you will have a proper time to work

through the chosen prayer points, it is most important to look for a good time, and a good location. Prayer is serious business that requires proper planning and concentration. I will suggest you set a certain time to do the praying. A minimum of thirty minutes in my opinion and experience should be set apart. Ideally, I will recommend one hour and multiples of one hour. The Lord Jesus Christ set time apart to pray – *Now in the morning, having risen a long while before daylight, He went out and departed to a solitary place; and there He prayed.* Mark 1: 35 The apostles of our Lord continued in the example that Christ left them – *Now Peter and John went up together to the temple at the hour of prayer, the ninth hour.* Acts 3: 1

Daniel, a Jewish top official in the Babylonian empire set aside time regularly to pray. *Now when Daniel knew that the writing was signed, he went home. And in his upper room, with his windows open toward Jerusalem, he knelt down on his knees three times that day, and prayed and gave thanks before his God, as was his custom since early days.* Daniel 6: 10

It is not legalism to set time apart to pray. Serious business requires diligent and concerted effort.

3. Start the prayer session with praise. This to some

long-standing Christians may look like the usual thing we say and possibly do. And there is the tendency to rush over this or do it just to tick the box and move on to more 'important' things. This error must be avoided by all means. Praise, if well done lifts your faith. God becomes bigger in your sight. Even before you utter the first word of prayer, there is already an assurance in your heart that 'it will be done', and very truly it will be done.

4. Each prayer declaration is preceded by a Bible verse. This is intentional. And the purpose is to establish the fact that the prayers are scriptural. Prayers that are based on the word of God will always get the attention of the Author of the word, and will strike fear into the heart of the enemy. Ecclesiastes 8:4 says: *Where the word of a king is, there is power; and who may say to him, What are you doing?*

5. The next step is to read through the particular block of prayer declarations. Read through at least twice. Let the meaning and gravity of the declaration soak in. After this, take each sentence and declare it. Build on each prayer declaration as you go along. Feel free to expand them and make them specific for your own circumstance and situation. Speak them out as much as it is practicable.

6. Read through the whole book. Listen out in the spirit for particular inspired word for your life. Hold on to such words and confess them over and over till it becomes flesh (comes alive and real to you). My covenant with God is that there is a WORD for everyone who will pick up this book to read. Don't miss yours!

7. Finally, give thanks to God for answered prayers. Do not be economical with your praise. Praise Him with passion and praise Him sincerely. Remember that you may have to go back to the prayers as often as it takes to have your answer.

CHAPTER THREE

HELP ME LORD

The first big blessing God gave the first man, Adam, was a helper. A person is only as good as the help available to him or her. God is the ultimate Helper who directs all sources of help in the universe. If He does not help a person, the person stays stranded and stuck.

A king in ancient Israel recognised that truth when a woman came to him in time of great trouble. His response is very telling:

*Then, as the king of Israel was passing by on the wall, a woman cried out to him, saying, **"Help, my lord, O king!"** And he said, **"If the LORD does not help you, where can I find help for you?** From the threshing floor or from the winepress?"* 2 Kings 6: 26–27

The very first words of declaration and confession shall be that God helps you and sends you help.

My Help Comes From The Lord

Psalm 121: 1 – 2 – *I will lift up my eyes to the hills—From whence comes my help? My help comes from the LORD, Who made heaven and earth.*

DECLARATION: I declare boldly and confidently that the living God only is my Help. I have no other source of help but from Him. Whatever help I receive comes from Jehovah. I have no other god but Elohim the God of Israel. I am not in agreement or covenant with any other, but the Lord God Almighty.

Any agreement made on my behalf to receive help from any other source are now cancelled and disannulled. I reject all forms of help from demons and ancestral spirits.

Whatever agreement I may have made knowingly or inadvertently to receive help from any power outside of God are hereby nullified in Jesus' name.

I command every help the Father has released to me to come to me now in Jesus' name. Wherever my help is held down or held back, I demand and command that all such help be released now in Jesus' name.

12

I am not helpless, because the Lord my God will help me. I am not hapless because Jehovah shall raise me up in Jesus' name. I am helped in Jesus' name! Amen.

Marvellously Helped

2 Chronicles 26: 15^b...*So his fame spread far and wide, for he was marvellously helped till he became strong.*

Psalm 20: 1-2 – *May the LORD answer you when you are in trouble! May the God of Jacob protect you! May he send you help from his Temple and give you aid from Mount Zion.*

DECLARATION: Father, send me my helpers of destiny today. Please make them selfless, secure, strong, seasoned and special; and don't let them ever change to opposers and destroyers of destiny in Jesus' name.

I command anything that may be keeping them in hiding to be torn off now in Jesus' name.

I hereby submit myself as a helper and partner of destiny to someone the Father has prepared. Father, raise us up for one another in your church in the name of Jesus. I am a helper and I myself shall be greatly helped in Jesus' name.

13

I am marvellously helped. Amen.

CHAPTER FOUR

MY LIFE SHALL PRAISE GOD

The number one duty of man is to worship God and show forth His glory by the life of dedication that we live. This section shall reinforce this very principle. The more you dedicate yourself to worship God, the more you will find yourself released and empowered to worship Him. Also remember that God is most glorified when we do well spiritually and in all other areas of our lives.

My Life of Praise

1 Peter 2: 9 (GNB) – *But you are the chosen race, the King's priests, the holy nation, God's own people, chosen to proclaim the wonderful acts of God, who called you out of darkness into his own marvellous light.*

DECLARATION: Father, I declare and affirm that as long as

I am alive, I will praise You. Your praise O Lord shall be my daily food and the worship of Your name shall be my delight. As you touch my eyes, I will see Your goodness and mercy in a new light; as You touch my lips, I will speak of Your love with new words I have never used before; as You touch my hands and feet, they shall clap and dance new dance in Jesus' name. Lord, I promise before the angels in heaven and Your people that YOUR praise shall never cease from my mouth in Jesus' name. I formally declare that I am an addict of Jehovah praise; and I shall never recover from the addiction of praise in Jesus' name.

Praise Pledge

Psalm 34: 1 – *I will bless the LORD at all times; His praise shall continually be in my mouth.*

DECLARATION: I hereby pledge and declare that the praise of God shall continually be in my mouth this year. No one shall stop my praise, and no situation will spoil my praise. Out of my innermost being shall proceed quality and abundant praise in Jesus' name.

By the special grace of God, my praise shall be genuine, fresh, loud, and it shall reach heaven in Jesus' name.

Praise shall meet praise in my mouth. While I am still thanking God for one thing, many more blessings will roll in Jesus' name. My life shall be the best advertisement of God's mercy and grace. This pledge and affirmation shall last my whole life in Jesus' mighty name. Amen!

Praise at All Cost

Hebrews 13: 15 – *Therefore by Him let us continually offer the sacrifice of praise to God, that is, the fruit of our lips, giving thanks to His name.*

DECLARATION: I declare in the name of Jesus that my number one preoccupation in life shall be to praise my God. By the special grace of my great Redeemer, I declare that the grace to pay the price of praise is mine in Jesus' name. I shall not faint or fall at the altar of praise, but in confidence and with joy I will offer my sacrifice of praise. Praise shall not be a chore, but a joy for me in Jesus' name. My praise shall not shrink, my praise shall not spoil and my praise shall not stop in Jesus' name. No distance will be too far for me to go and praise God. No price will be too great for me to pay to praise my God, and no effort will be too much to make to give the praise that is due to my God in Jesus' name. I shall praise God at all cost in Jesus' name!

Joyous Praise

Psalm 149: 5 – *Let the saints be joyful in glory; Let them sing aloud on their beds.*

DECLARATION: With my mouth I will praise my God and Maker. I declare in the name of Jesus that my praise shall never be a grudging praise; my adoration of my King shall be all enrapturing.
I will never praise or worship my God secretly but openly for all to hear and see.

Early in the morning I will praise my dear Lord and Keeper. I will go to bed at night with a thankful heart and with loud praise on my lips. While still on my bed in the morning, I shall wake up to praise in Jesus' name.

By the mercies of the Lord, I shall receive grace to praise my dear Lord and King joyously and enthusiastically. Half-hearted praise shall not for once be heard from my lips in Jesus' name.

I shall sing the praise of my good Father excitedly, and the devil shall not be able to do anything about it in Jesus' name.

Increasing Praise

Psalm 149: 6 – *Let the high praises of God be in their mouth, And a two-edged sword in their hand.*

DECLARATION: By the great grace of my Lord and God, I declare boldly that my praise grow faster than my age. I shall not know a better yesterday in my life of praise. As there is no limit to the height of the heaven, so shall there be no limit to my ever-increasing praise in Jesus' name.

As my Lord Jesus grew in grace and in favour daily, so shall I grow in praise and worship daily in Jesus' name. In my praise life, I am unstoppable, unconquerable, and irrepressible in Jesus' name. O my mouth, I command you to open wider in praise daily, I command you to speak louder of the goodness of the Lord and I instruct you to sing more clearly of the love of Jesus. My cup of praise shall be full and overflow and yet it shall never stop in Jesus' name.

Praise of God is what I love, and the high and highest praise of Jehovah I shall have reasons to sing all my days in Jesus' name. Sing my voice, speak my mouth, clap my hands and dance my feet for the great God who has been so good to you.

Unending Praise

Psalm 34:1 – *I will bless the LORD at all times; His praise shall continually be in my mouth.*

DECLARATION: The river of God's praise welling up within me shall never run dry. Praise shall birth more praise in my mouth in Jesus' name. The word of my mouth shall never be words of murmuring or grumbling but shall be effortless words of glorious praise to my God. As I walk through life, in easy and difficult times, praise of my God shall be my vehicle that will transport me into the place of victory and triumph in Jesus' name.

I will not lose my praise; I will not leave my praise behind and I shall not lease out my praise for any reason in Jesus' name.

Dedicated to My God in Prayer

Romans 12:1 – *I beseech you therefore, brethren, by the mercies of God, that you present your bodies a living sacrifice, holy, acceptable to God, which is your reasonable service.*

Acts 6:4 – *But we will give ourselves continually to prayer and to the ministry of the word.*

DECLARATION: Father, I offer my heart, my intellect, my lips, my tongue, my limbs (arms to raise, feet to walk, and knees to kneel) unto you right now. Take them and use them for the purpose of prayer. From now on, I shall get better in prayer daily. From now on, in the name of Jesus I shall love prayer. From now on, my prayers shall return with results in the name of Jesus. My testimonies shall encourage many to pray. By the mercies of the Lord, I shall a walking testimony of answered prayers in the name of Jesus. Amen.

My God is Big

Jeremiah 32:17 – *"Ah Lord GOD! behold, thou hast made the heaven and the earth by thy great power and stretched out arm, and there is nothing too hard for thee."*

DECLARATION: I declare that the God of Abraham, Isaac and Jacob, the Father of our Lord Jesus Christ is my God! I know and I declare boldly that nothing is too hard for my God. I declare that my life situation is a very small matter for Him to resolve. My God is the greatest, wisest, kindest of all. He is my Father. Thank You Lord Jesus for being my God.

CHAPTER FIVE

I AM A COVENANT CHILD

The God of covenant whom we serve has bound Himself over to fulfilling all the great promises He has made to us. It is important that we 'remind' Him of the promises made to us.

Covenant Prayer

Psalm 89: 33-34 – *Nevertheless My loving kindness I will not utterly take from him, Nor allow My faithfulness to fail. My covenant I will not break, Nor alter the word that has gone out of My lips.*

DECLARATION: I am a child of covenant (promise), therefore the devil and any form of evil shall not have control over me. I shall be cheerful because Jesus has overcome the powers of the world on my behalf. (John 16: 33). As He has promised, Satan shall be crushed under my feet very soon in Jesus' name. (Romans 16: 20).

The experience of salvation is the helmet cover for my head, the protection for my chest (my heart, my breathe) is His righteousness. By the glittering cover of His righteousness, the enemy shall be blinded. The truth of the word of God is a tie on my waist, holding my armour together and intact. The shield of faith and absolute trust in Jesus is a mobile impenetrable wall shielding me from the arrows of the enemy. The word of God in my mouth is a lethal weapon against the devil. By the preaching of the gospel, I shall tread on serpents and scorpions in Jesus' name.

Because my dear Saviour the Lord Jesus has promised me, I shall reign with Him eternally. The place He has gone to prepare for me, I shall enter into and my reward I shall not lose in the name of Jesus.

Freed from Family Sins & Transgressions

Isaiah 43:25 – *I, even I, am He who blots out your transgressions for My own sake; And I will not remember your sins.*

DECLARATION: Father, according to Your word, please blot out all my sins of this and previous years for Your name sake. Every accusation against me is hereby nullified in Jesus' name. I shall have no carry over of sin, error and iniquity. Every ancestral sin and every trait of family weakness and failing shall be buried from this moment forward in Jesus name. I am loosed from the grip of generational sin in Jesus' name. Sin and its power shall not dominate me. From now on, I shall live the life of Christ who dwells in me and my life shall be a praise to my God. Amen.

I Shall Not Suffer Shame

Isaiah 54:4 – *"Do not fear, for you will not be ashamed; Neither be disgraced, for you will not be put to shame; For you will forget the shame of your youth, And will not remember the reproach of your widowhood anymore.*

DECLARATION: I stand on the word of God and I declare that I will not be ashamed. All past shame in my life shall be no more. In place of shame, I will have glory; in place of reproach, I will be celebrated in Jesus' name.

The days of hiding are over and the days of coming out are here in Jesus' name. I declare in the name of Jesus that I am not forsaken or abandoned, but I am loved by the Father of glory. All who are rejoicing over my stumbling shall see me rise again and they shall fear my God who has lifted me up. My sun shall never set in Jesus' name.

Peace and Life

Malachi 2:5 – *My covenant was with him, one of life and peace, And I gave them to him that he might fear Me; So he feared Me And was reverent before My name.*

DECLARATION: I declare that I am under God's covenant of life; therefore I shall not die (spiritually, emotionally, materially), but I shall live in Jesus' name. Whatever is dead in my life shall come back alive now, in Jesus' name.

I declare in the name of Jesus that I am under God's covenant of peace; therefore all stormy waters in my life shall be still. I am an agent of peace, therefore from now on, let no one trouble me.

Through me, the message of peace shall be published, and many shall bow to the Prince of peace in Jesus' name. In peace I will end this year, and in peace I will live the rest of my life in Jesus' name.

I have The Victory

1 Corinthians 15:57 – *But thanks be to God, who gives us the victory through our Lord Jesus Christ.*

DECLARATION: Father God, we thank you because you have given us the victory. By the power in the name of Jesus Christ, the Lion of the tribe of Judah, I declare that I am undefeatable, unconquerable and I am totally and permanently victorious in Jesus' name.

Any poison of doubt and discouragement that may be in my life is hereby neutralised by the powerful blood of Jesus. Failure shall be far from me this year and success shall be my daily experience in Jesus' name.

Every demonic assignment against my peace and the peace of my family, church and community are declared 'failed' in Jesus' name. I am victorious in Jesus' name!

I Shall Not Diminish

Jeremiah 30:19 – *Then out of them shall proceed thanksgiving and the voice of those who make merry; I will multiply them, and they shall not diminish; I will also glorify them, and they shall not be small.*

DECLARATION: I declare in the name of Jesus that I shall not decrease; I shall not diminish, I shall not decay and my life shall not be deformed. BUT...

I shall multiply, I shall increase, and I shall flourish. There shall be no stopping or stalling to my progress in Jesus' name. As Jesus increased in all areas, so shall I increase. My growth shall defy all predictions, my increase and enlargement shall be unprecedented. These are my declarations and they are settled forever in Jesus' name. Amen.

My Expectation Shall Not Be Cut Off

Proverbs 23:18 – *For surely there is an end; and thine expectation shall not be cut off.*

Psalms 62: 5 (NLT) – *Let all that I am wait quietly before God, for my hope is in him.*

DECLARATION: Father, birth in me a lively hope today. I reject every form of discouragement that makes a person give up hope and expectation. I am from this moment entering into a high state of alert and expectation in Jesus' name. There shall be no more blankness of mind, fuzziness of idea or glazing of my eyes in the name of Jesus.

I declare that my vision of (spiritual growth, job, marriage, financial freedom, ministry etc.) are clear and sharp in Jesus' name. I am expectant in the name of Jesus! *(three times).* I am expecting in the name of Jesus!! *(three times)*

I Am on Time

Habakkuk 2:3 – *Put it in writing, because it is not yet time for it to come true. But the time is coming quickly, and what I show you will come true. It may seem slow in coming but wait for it; it will certainly take place, and it will not be delayed.*

DECLARATION: My times are in Your hands O Lord my God; please deliver me from failure.

Father, guide me with power, guide me with precision, and guide me with providence to my place of abundant harvest in Jesus' name. By the special grace of God, I shall not be too late, and I shall not be too early, but I shall be exactly on time for the abundant harvest the Father has prepared for me. I will not miss my bus; I will not miss my train and I shall not miss my flight. I shall be ready for the final flight home in Jesus' name.

Holy Spirit Fire in My Bones

Jeremiah 20:9 – *Then I said, "I will not make mention of Him, Nor speak anymore in His name." But His word was in my heart* *like a burning fire Shut up in my bones; I was weary of holding it back, And I could not.*

DECLARATION: I receive a special passion for prayer today in Jesus' name. Fire of prayer – be kindled in me today in Jesus' name! My bones, flesh and blood shall only find rest in God as I draw close to Him in prayer. Father, let all evil complacency be banished in my life today.

I shall lose all appetite for useless conversations, contemplation and consumption in Jesus' name. Let a righteous hunger for prayer arise within me now in Jesus' name. I will wake up hungry for prayer, and I shall go to bed satisfied and filled with answers to prayers in Jesus' name. I am a man/woman of prayer in Jesus' name!

CHAPTER SIX

EVER INCREASING GLORY

The Glory Is Here

Isaiah 60:1 – *Arise, shine; For your light has come! And the glory of the LORD is risen upon you.*

DECLARATION: I declare according to scriptures that the day of revealing of God's glory in my life shall not be delayed any longer. I declare that as I arise, my Father's glory shall be seen all over and around me. I declare in the name of Jesus that from now on, the life I shall live shall be by the grace of the Son of God who died and rose for me. I declare that I and my children shall be for God's glorious wonders in this generation.

I declare in the name of my Lord Jesus Christ that these words I have spoken shall be done. I stand on the living word of God which says: "As I live," says the LORD, "just as you have spoken in My hearing, so I will do to you." So let it be, Lord. Thank you, Lord. Amen!

I am Made for God's Glory

Isaiah 43:7 – *Even every one that is called by my name: for I have created him for my glory, I have formed him; yea, I have made him.*

DECLARATION: I declare according to scripture that I am a child of glory, made to show forth the glory of God to this generation. I receive strength to shine brighter and brighter by the day. People shall see me and give glory to God for my life. The glory of God over my life shall be a rebuke and a terror to the enemy and all his powers. The glory of God over my life shall not diminish, nor be distorted, but shall dominate my surrounding and community in Jesus' name. For all I am, and for all I will ever be, God alone shall be praised, and all the glory shall be unto El-Elyon alone. Amen.

From Glory to Glory

2 Corinthians 3:18 – *But we all, with unveiled face, beholding as in a mirror the glory of the Lord, are being transformed into the same image from glory to glory, just as by the Spirit of the Lord.*

DECLARATION: The Lord has spoken good concerning me; I shall be changed from glory to glory in Jesus' name. In the name of Jesus, right now I am being changed from glory to glory. My past is past, my present is glorious, and my future is beautiful in Jesus' name. My change has come, my change is here, and my change is coming in Jesus' name. All the days of my life, I shall wait patiently until I am fully changed to be like Jesus. (Job 14:14)

What the world sees is not all there is to me, a glorious change is coming into my life, into my family, into my church family, into the body of Christ and into my community.

The night is past, a glorious dawn has come, and the beauty of the Lord shall be seen over me in Jesus' name. The wind is blowing, my change has come, and my God is glorified. Hallelujah! Amen!!!

I command that every contrary wind working against the glory of God in my life (family, church, community), cease now in Jesus' name.

My destiny is not for debate. He who called me shall see me safely home. I am a child of Destiny; the wind of the Holy Spirit is carrying me and I shall be unstoppable in Jesus' name.

Lift up your heads O you gates, and be lifted up you ancient doors and let the King of glory who is carrying me go in. Into my place of enlargement, expansion, growth, and miraculous wonders I shall go in Jesus' name. I am above and not beneath, I am light and not darkness, I am progressing and not stagnant, AND I am blessed and not cursed in Jesus' name.

The devil is subdued under me and he is crushed under me in the name of Jesus (*And the God of peace will crush Satan under your feet shortly.* Romans 16:20). I am victorious in the name of Jesus. My change has come! Hallelujah!! Amen!!!

The 7-Fold Spirit of God

Isaiah 11 1-2 – *There shall come forth a Rod from the stem of Jesse, And a Branch shall grow out of his roots. The Spirit of the LORD shall rest upon Him, The Spirit of wisdom and understanding, The Spirit of counsel and might, The Spirit of knowledge and of the fear of the LORD.*

DECLARATION: I declare that from now on the seven-fold Spirit of God shall regularly manifest in me. The Spirit of God in me shall be seen by all as the evidence of the in-dwelling Person of Christ in me. The spirit of wisdom and understanding shall make me wiser than my instructors in Jesus' name. In wisdom

I shall go out and make war and in wisdom I shall celebrate my God-given victory.

By the spirit of knowledge and the fear of the Lord I shall be numbered among those who know their God and do exploits. The fear of the Lord shall preserve me, and I shall not stumble or fall in Jesus' name.

Spirit of The Lord Rest on Me

CONFESSION: I confess that the Spirit of the Lord rests on me and my household. The same Spirit that raised Jesus from the dead shall daily give life to my body in Jesus' name. By the Spirit of the Lord, I shall overcome and overpower the spirit of the world and the spirit of the age. I am subject to the Spirit of the Lord and to no other spirit in Jesus' name. By the virtue of the mark of Spirit of Jehovah upon me, I declare–let no one trouble me in Jesus' name. Because I am a carrier of the Spirit of the Lord, I demand that all contrary spirits shall bow and flee at my command in Jesus' name.

Filled with The Spirit of Wisdom

DECLARATION: I declare in the name of Jesus that folly shall not be found in me, but abundance of wisdom. I am wise because I fear the Lord, I am wise because the law of the Lord is my delight. By the help of the Spirit of the Lord, I shall walk in wisdom and find my place amongst wise people in Jesus' name.

I declare that the deposit of wisdom in my life shall never run dry and the repository of wise acts shall daily increase in Jesus' name. I am wise and I will only do wise things in Jesus' name. The spirit of wisdom resting upon me shall never lift in Jesus' name. I am filled by the Spirit of wisdom in Jesus' name.

Walking in The Spirit of Understanding

DECLARATION: I receive the Spirit of Jehovah to understand things and situations quickly and fully. As Christ surprised those who were ahead of Him, so shall all those over and above me be surprised at the display of godly understanding that shall be displayed by me in Jesus' name. I shall not walk in darkness or in confusion because the power to understand dark and hidden matters shall fully rest upon me in Jesus' name. Because I have understanding, I shall receive favour in Jesus' name.

By The Spirit of Counsel, I Shall Rule

DECLARATION: I receive grace to manifest the work of the Spirit of counsel. I shall not drift or remain undecided. By the working of the Spirit of counsel, I shall be blessed, and I shall be a blessing to my family, to the Church of Jesus Christ and to my world. Where there is confusion, I shall bring clarity; where there is wavering, I shall be an agent of stability in Jesus' name. Out of my mouth shall proceed words of sound counsel, and nations shall find hope though the pronouncements of my mouth in Jesus' name.

I am full of the Spirit of Counsel! Amen.

Prevailing by The Spirit of Might

DECLARATION: Because I am girded with strength, I hereby declare that I am strong and courageous in Jesus' name. In the face of opposition, I shall stand and not buckle. Despair, disappointment, and depression shall be far from me.

I am stronger than the enemy, wiser than the adversary and I am better than my opponents in Jesus' name. The strength to carry through and fulfil my God ordained destiny shall be mine in Jesus' name. The Spirit of might shall manifest fully in me in the morning, in the afternoon and at night.

I am strong in Jesus' name! Amen

Distinguished by The Spirit of Knowledge

DECLARATION: I declare that by the Spirit of knowledge I shall know the ways of God. I shall not walk in ignorance but in the knowledge of the truth of God. I choose the way of the knowledge of the Holy Spirit over the knowledge of this world. I shall not diminish in knowledge neither shall I be deprived of the necessary knowledge of God in Jesus' name. My quest for the pure knowledge of God shall not decrease but increase daily in Jesus' name. I declare that from the fountain of the knowledge of God I shall drink all my days in Jesus' name. The Spirit of knowledge upon me shall cause me to know the deep things of God in Jesus' name. I am set apart to know what is hard to know, and to know what is hidden in Jesus' name.

Spirit of Fear of The Lord Rest on Me Now!

DECLARATION: I declare that by the virtue of my union with Christ Jesus, I am filled with the Spirit of the fear of the Lord. All my days, I shall fear no other but my God, in Jesus' name. I shall never lose my fear of God but shall daily be in awe of Him who gave me breath in Jesus' name. By the fear of the Lord, all opposition shall fear me and bow in Jesus' name. Strangers shall hear of me and tremble and run out of their hideouts in Jesus' name. Because I bow to my God, situations and the forces of the enemy shall bow to me in Jesus' name. I am free from the fear of men that ensnares, I am liberated from the fear of death that incarcerates in Jesus' name. All my days I shall walk in the fear of the Lord in Jesus' name.

CHAPTER SEVEN

THE ENEMY IS SUBDUED

Evil Weapon Shall Fail 1

Isaiah 54:17 – *No weapon formed against you shall prosper, And every tongue which rises against you in judgment You shall condemn. This is the heritage of the servants of the LORD, And their righteousness is from Me, says the LORD.*

DECLARATION: I hereby align myself with the word of God and I declare that no weapon crafted against me shall prosper. The forces of the enemy working against me from within and from without, from my past and in the present shall utterly fail in Jesus' name. The reign of sin, sickness, and suffering is over and a new dawn of freedom from all evil has broken in our lives in Jesus' name. I shall not fear the terror by night neither will the arrow of the enemy that fly in daytime strike me. Because of the Father's love for me, I shall be delivered from all attacks of the enemy in Jesus' name. Amen.

Evil Weapon Shall Fail 2

Isaiah 44:25 – *Thus says the LORD, your Redeemer, And He who formed you from the womb: "I am the LORD, who makes all things, Who stretches out the heavens all alone, Who spreads abroad the earth by Myself; Who frustrates the signs of the babblers, And drives diviners mad; Who turns wise men backward, And makes their knowledge foolishness;*

DECLARATION: I declare in the name of Jesus that all plans contrary to the will of God for my life shall meet with frustration and stiff opposition. I am joined to Jesus Christ my Lord as a co-heir of God, and I shall not be defeated. Every voice of accusation raised against me (my family, the church of God) shall be silenced. The gathering of opponents of God set against my life shall scatter. Angels at my Father's command shall fight for me and the enemy shall be confounded in Jesus' name. I hereby confidently declare that I shall not be defeated in Jesus' name.

I Will Recover All

1 Samuel 30:8 – *So David inquired of the LORD, saying, "Shall*

I pursue this troop? Shall I overtake them?" And He answered him, "Pursue, for you shall surely overtake them and without fail recover all."

DECLARATION: By the mercies of God, I declare that every blessing I have lost through my carelessness, through the callousness of the enemy or by the correction of my God, shall be fully restored in Jesus' name. By the word of God, I recover all! I recover all and completely in Jesus' name.

According to the authority given to me as a child of the Most High God, I command all doors of blessings shut against me to be opened in Jesus' name. "Open up, ancient gates! Open up, ancient doors, and let the King of glory enter." Psalm 24: 7 NLT

I declare in the name of Jesus that the door of service to this community opened to us shall remain open. I command every opponent of the gospel in this nation to go blind in Jesus' name. (Acts 13: 8–12, Acts 9: 8).

I recover every lost key, every buried key and every hidden key to my door of advancement in Jesus' name. I recover all! With the master key of David, let all doors of God's treasure house of blessing be opened to me, my family and the church in Jesus' name. Amen

Come Back Alive

Ezekiel 37:10 – *So I prophesied as He commanded me, and breath came into them, and they lived, and stood upon their feet, an exceedingly great army.*

DECLARATION: Whatever thing in my life that is dead but ought to be living shall come alive now in the name of Jesus. I ask in the name of Jesus that the same power which raised my Saviour from the dead, shall give life to my physical body, to my ministry, to my children, my finances, my spiritual life etc. and I shall be full of life in the name of Jesus.

Nothing good in my hand shall die, but rather shall go from strength to strength in Jesus' name. Whatever is dying or dead in my life, I command you again, come back alive fully in Jesus' name.

Everything that is dead which ought to be alive in my community shall come alive now. The spirit of repentance shall come back alive in my community. Every form of moral decadence and pride shall die, and the spirit of holiness and the fear of the Lord shall come alive in our nation and nations in Jesus' name.

CHAPTER EIGHT

MY PAST IS PAST, MY FUTURE IS BEAUTIFUL

Out of Prison

Isaiah 42:6-7 – *"I, the LORD, have called You in righteousness, And will hold Your hand; I will keep You and give You as a covenant to the people, As a light to the Gentiles, To open blind eyes, To bring out prisoners from the prison, Those who sit in darkness from the prison house."*

DECLARATION: I declare that by the power of my God, I am coming out of the prison in the name of Jesus. I declare in the name of Jesus that whatsoever area of life I am bound I shall be made totally and completely free right now.

I command every chain that binds my hands to be loosed now

in Jesus' name. My hands are now free to do good works and mighty exploits in Jesus' name.

I command every shackle that binds my feet to be loosed now in Jesus' name. My feet are free to step into the glorious place of my destiny in Jesus' name.

I command every rope tying my mind to be loosed now in Jesus' name. I am free from every unfruitful and depressive thoughts in Jesus' name. The Lord who sent His angel to release Peter from the prison, please send your angels today to release and lead me out of prison today in the name of Jesus. I shall never be bound ever again in the name of Jesus.

I am free in Christ Jesus and I am free indeed. Hallelujah!

Generational Demarcation from My Ancestors Sins

Jeremiah 31:29 (GNB) – *When that time comes, people will no longer say, "The parents ate the sour grapes, But the children got the sour taste."*

DECLARATION: Father Lord, I am aware of your word which says that you punish the sins of the ancestors to the third and fourth generation, but you also say in your infallible word that you show mercy to thousands of them who love you and keep your commandments. I hereby stand on your word and say: Father, please show me mercy, show us mercy. Let the sins of our ancestors be not visited over us in Jesus' name. I and my brothers and sisters hereby come under the cover of the blood of Jesus. Let the right reward for all our sins fall on the crucified Saviour and in the name of Jesus we are free.

I hereby come under the covenant of generational demarcation of sin, and by the mercy of the Lord; I shall not suffer for my ancestors' sins in Jesus' name.

Every ancestral fountain of sorrow and failure shall dry up in my life in Jesus' name. From the fountain of life, I shall drink and out of the overflowing cup of blessing of my Father I shall be refreshed in Jesus' name. I declare according to the word of God that I shall not have the sour taste of the sour grapes that my ancestors ate in Jesus' name. Every iniquity of my ancestors is now buried never to reappear in my life in Jesus' name. Thank you Jesus.

Freedom from Divinations

Number 23:23 – *"For there is no sorcery against Jacob, Nor any* divination against Israel. It now must be said of Jacob And of Israel, 'Oh, what God has done!'"

DECLARATION: Father, in the name of Jesus, I take your word in my mouth and declare that no divination against me shall stand. Every arrow sent to wound me (wound us) shall be sent back in the name of Jesus. I neutralise every poisoned arrow shot at me by the blood of Jesus. No evil arrow shall have any impact on me in the name of Jesus. By the power in the name of Jesus, I ask that the soothing healing oil of the Holy Spirit be poured onto any wound I may have. I hereby receive healing right now in the name of Jesus. The balm of Gilead shall work for me in the name of Jesus.

I decree that all forms of images raised against us (me) in our dreams be blurred and blotted out in the name of Jesus. Every effigy made to afflict me shall fail to connect with me in the name of Jesus. My name shall be too hot for the enemy to toy with. I retrieve all forms of my image in the occult world and I hide them inside the name of my God in Jesus' name.

I destroy all links between my body and those of evil sacrificial animals in the name of Jesus. My body is the temple of God, and those that destroy the Lord's temple, the Lord shall destroy;

therefore let the word of God take effect now against all who seek to destroy my body in the name of Jesus. All forms of sickness shall be far from us in the name of Jesus.

Divine Fulfilment – Bless Me Lord!

1 Kings 8:56 – *"Blessed be the LORD, who has given rest to His people Israel, according to all that He promised. There has not failed one word of all His good promise, which He promised through His servant Moses."*

DECLARATION: I demand in the name of Jesus that all the good promises of the Lord shall come to pass in my life (our lives). Every pending promise of job, financial breakthrough, marriages, healing and health, ministry success and spiritual wholeness come alive right now in Jesus' name. Today, I will not let You go until You bless me. Bless me Lord, bless me, bless me and restore back to me all lost opportunities. Today, I shall know fulfilment and never come short again in the name of Jesus.

I am a child of the Kingdom, and I hereby declare that I shall exercise the dominion the King has given me. I shall not be dominated by situations, circumstances or demonic forces in the name of Jesus. No adverse situation shall rule over me, but all adversity shall turn into advancement for me in the name of Jesus. Though the enemies come against me in one way, they shall flee in seven ways.

Every stumbling block put in my way, shall turn into stepping stones in Jesus' name. Every gate erected to shut me in shall turn to doors of opportunity into my destiny. I am strong and not weak, I am above and not beneath. Because I am washed by the blood, I am not washed up neither I am wishy washy. In the name that is above all names, I declare boldly that my journey shall not end in the pit, but in the palace where I will continue to exercise dominion with the King of kings. Amen.

CHAPTER NINE

REDEEMED FROM HEAD TO TOE

Be Lifted O My Head!

Psalms 3:3 – *But thou, O LORD, art a shield for me; my glory, and the lifter up of mine head.*

DECLARATION: I declare that my head is ultimately submitted unto no one but Christ Jesus my Lord. All ancestral and acquired negative power are hereby commanded to get off my head in Jesus' name. I renounce and reject every authority under which I have put my head knowingly or inadvertently. All evil hands ever laid on my head are hereby commanded to be removed. I remove my head from under your control right now.

All evil hand pressing my head down are hereby commanded to be removed now. My head shall be lifted up and shall not be bowed.

Evil burden secretly dropped on my head are commanded to roll off now in Jesus' name. My head shall never again hang in shame or in sorrow in the mighty name of Jesus. The Lord who raised the head of Joseph from shame and oppression shall lift my head up in Jesus' name.

My forehead is hereby made to be stronger and harder than those of my opponents and adversaries in Jesus' name. Like adamant that is harder than flint so shall my head be against my enemies in the name of Jesus Christ my Saviour. (*Like adamant stone, harder than flint, I have made your forehead; do not be afraid of them, nor be dismayed at their looks, though they are a rebellious house. Ezekiel 3: 9*)

The crowns that my Father has prepared for me, my head will wear them in Jesus' name.

My head, I command you–be still and receive your crowns now in Jesus' name.

My head is under the authority of Jehovah God. It shall not bow to any other god. My head is sacred and sanctified. No curse shall ever rest on this head. No strange load shall be carried on my head. My head is blessed and not cursed. Every force trying to keep my head down shall be broken.

Above all adversaries my head shall be raised. The oil of anointing on my head shall not run dry. The glory of God upon my head shall not depart.

I declare in the name of Jesus that my head shall be lifted. I shall not walk with bowed head.

I command you my head, attract favour, attract blessings in Jesus' name. I command you my head, reject failure, reject shame, reject retrogression in a Jesus name. I declare in the name of the Lord that my head shall not be a dumping ground for disease, disasters, demons and destruction; rather joy, victory, peace shall find a resting place on my head.

I declare in the name of the Lord that anything evil targeting my head shall be diverted. Wherever I go, I pronounce that my head shall tower above many others. In humility I shall be honoured, in meekness I shall possess. All lingering attack over my head are hereby commanded to disperse and be destroyed now in Jesus name. My head, I say to you, you shall reach the place God has ordained for you in Jesus' name.

My head, I say to you again—you are sacred and blessed in Jesus' name.

My Eyes Shall See No Evil

Ephesians 1:18 – *The eyes of your understanding being enlightened; that you may know what is the hope of His calling, what are the riches of the glory of His inheritance in the saints.*

DECLARATION: I covenant with you my eyes that you shall not behold evil or stare at iniquity. My eyes are not evil but good. I shall see the best in people and my heart shall respond with love in Jesus' name.

By the power of God, my inner eyes shall be opened to understand mysteries and deep things of God.

My eyes shall see great visions that will benefit my generation and the coming generations. The light of God shall shine on my path, and I will see clearly where He is leading me in Jesus' name.

My eye shall not see anything that will grieve me neither will it look back in regret. Day by day, I shall see God's glory, and I shall behold His wonders in Jesus' name.

I reject anything designed to cause me pain through my eyes.

By the mercies of God, I will not see (witness) my children's funeral.

Every spiritual, physical and emotional weakness in my eyes shall be changed to strength in Jesus' name.

From now on, my eyes shall be quick to identify opportunities– Gospel opportunities, business opportunities, and all good opportunities shall not pass me by in Jesus' name.

I hereby dedicate my eyes to Jesus my Lord. My eyes shall not behold iniquity neither will you admire sin and unrighteousness. Only good and the beauty of holiness you will see until you see Jesus face to face.

My eyes are ordained and appointed to see miracles and goodness of the Lord in the land of the living. My eyes are hereby commanded–You shall see nothing ugly and shameful. The ugliness of sin shall be resented and rejected by my eyes in Jesus' name. It shall not be said of me that my eyes are full of anything else but the righteousness of my God in Jesus' name.

By the power of the Holy Spirit I declare that my eyes shall be quick in picking out those requiring my Father's help in Jesus' name. My eyes shall work for my God and not for the enemy of my soul. I reject and renounce all the filth that the world is trying to feed my soul through my eyes.

By the special grace of my God, I hereby covenant with my eyes that you will not admire sin or desire what does not belong to you in Jesus' name.

My eyes shall not see disgrace nor will they behold my decline or fall from grace in Jesus' name. My God shall have mercy on me, so that I will not see my children buried in Jesus' name.

My eyes shall be anointed to see glorious visions and receive messages of greatness and deliverance for my household and my community.

By the kindness of the Lord, my eyes shall stay sharp and not dim in Jesus' name.

My Ears Shall Hear Good and Well

Job 12:10-11 – *The life of every living creature and the spirit in every human body are in his hands. Doesn't the ear distinguish sounds and the tongue taste food?*

Isaiah 50:5 – *The Almighty LORD will open my ears. I will not rebel, nor will I turn away from him.*

Matthew 13:16–*Blessed are your eyes because they see and your ears because they hear.*

Exodus 21:5-6 – But *if he makes this statement: I hereby declare my love for my master, my wife, and my children. I don't want to leave as a free man, then his master must bring him to God. The master must bring him to the door or the doorframe and pierce his ear with an awl. Then he will be his slave for life.*

DECLARATION: My ears belong to the Lord, and they shall only be used for His glory. I declare in the name of Jesus that my ears are totally dedicated to Jehovah as a symbol of my life dedication. My ears are not for gossips, my ears are not for slanderous reports about others, my ears are to hear good testimonies in Jesus' name.

I declare in the name of Jesus that my ears shall be discerning ears. No one shall fool me by their words because my ears are ordained and trained to distinguish right from wrong and evil from good in the name of Jesus.

Spiritual noises and cacophonies shall not have a place in my ears in Jesus' name. Peaceful words of God shall find my ears and settle there in Jesus' name.

From today, I command you my ears, you shall not receive bad news, neither will news of sorrow and disaster be yours. Though I ear strange news from afar, they shall not be mine in Jesus' name.

Father, I declare in the name of Jesus that according to your word, You will open my ears, and I will not rebel against you in Jesus' name.

I declare that I am not deaf spiritually, and I shall not be deaf physically in Jesus' name. I am emotionally sensitive to the cries of the world around me. My ears shall instruct my heart to feel for others and respond like my Saviour in Jesus' name.

My ears shall have no other function but to hear instructions and words of life from my Father and Maker in Jesus' name. My ears shall be inclined unto my dear Father moment by moment all the days of my life in Jesus' name. My ears, I demand of you that you will not hear the voice of the enemy, but that of Jesus Christ the Lord.

I covenant with my ears that you will not be attentive to lies of the enemy nor will you be attuned to the words of death and destruction in Jesus' name.

My ears, hear me now, I demand of you to be unresponsive and deaf to words of discouragement and despondency from the camp of the enemy in Jesus' name. My ears shall not receive or accept words of deception from the enemy in the mighty of Jesus.

In the name of Jesus, I hereby reject news of sorrow and disappointment. My ears are ordained to hear good news and testimonies of the faithfulness of the Lord.

By the hearing of the word of God, my faith shall grow and my progress shall be evident to all in Jesus' name.

My ears are blessed for hearing the word of God and they shall stay blessed in Jesus' name.

My Tongue is For Life and Healing

Job 5:21 – *You shall be hidden from the scourge of the tongue, And you shall not be afraid of destruction when it comes. (For your iniquity teaches your mouth, And you choose the tongue of the crafty.* **Job 15:5***)*

Isaiah 54:17 – *"No weapon formed against you shall prosper, And every tongue which rises against you in judgment You shall condemn. This is the heritage of the servants of the LORD, And their righteousness is from Me," says the LORD.*

Job 6:24 – *"Teach me, and I will hold my tongue; Cause me to understand wherein I have erred."*

Isaiah 50:4 – *The Lord GOD has given Me The tongue of the learned, That I should know how to speak A word in season to him who is weary. He awakens Me morning by morning, He awakens My ear to hear as the learned.*

Zephaniah 3:13 – *The remnant of Israel shall do no unrighteousness And speak no lies, Nor shall a deceitful tongue be found in their mouth; For they shall feed their flocks and lie down, And no one shall make them afraid.*

DECLARATION: I declare in the name of Jesus that I shall be hidden from the scourge of the tongue. I am not available for tongue-lashing because the Father shall hide me. The tongue of the crafty shall be far from me in Jesus' name, and when they come near, they shall be fully neutralised in Jesus' name.

Every weaponised tongue that rises against me shall utterly

fail in Jesus' name. According to the authority of the word of God, I hereby judge and condemn every tongue that rises against me, and any and every tongue that shall rise up against me in Jesus' name.

I receive instructions and teachings in holding my tongue. My all-wise Father is my coach and mentor. From now on, the grace to be discreet, discerning and deft with my tongue is mine in Jesus' name. I shall not be flippant with my tongue and my tongue shall only speak wise words in Jesus' name.

I declare in the name of Jesus that the Lord has given me the tongue of the learned. By the great power of God, I shall speak words of wisdom beyond my age, experience or training in Jesus' name. When people hear me speak, they shall marvel at the depth of godly wisdom that my tongue utters.

I receive the power and the grace to speak to those who are weary, tired and in trouble. My tongue is for healing and not for wounding in Jesus' name.

By the hearing of the ear, I shall learn wisdom and by the speaking of the tongue I shall dispense grace and love. I am a child of God set apart to bring joy and hope. My tongue I command you in the name of Jesus to go to work today, and bring life to this world. Amen!

I declare in the name of Jesus that I shall not be tongue-tied. Whenever and wherever answer is required and demanded of me, the great power of the Holy Spirit shall come upon me and I will confound my adversary and confuse my enemies in Jesus' name.

Whenever I am called upon to make a case for myself and above all for my Father's kingdom, I shall not be tongue-tied but bold in word and strong in conviction in Jesus' name. By the workings of the great power of God, the cloven tongue of fire of God shall rest on my head, and the words of my tongue shall be like holy fire consuming every opposition and blasphemy in Jesus' name. Amen

I hereby declare that my tongue is fully dedicated to the Lord and shall never speak lies in Jesus' name. There shall be no deceitful tongue in me. By my tongue my household shall be fed the living word of God in Jesus' name. I have the tongue of the learned in Jesus' name. Amen.

Pure and Strong Heart

Proverbs 4:23 – *"Keep your heart with all diligence, For out of*

it spring the issues of life. "

Ezekiel 36:26 – *I will give you a new heart and put a new spirit within you; I will take the heart of stone out of your flesh and give you a heart of flesh.*

DECLARATION: My heart is under the control of the Holy Spirit of God. Christ is the King on the throne of my heart. My heavenly Father holds the key to my heart. All forms of impurity and filth are hereby commanded to leave my heart. My heart is dedicated to the glory and praise of God. By the power of the Holy Spirit and by the washing of the blood of Christ, my heart is hereby commanded to be purged of dregs and dross in Jesus' name. By this my confession, and by the working of the word of God, I mandated my heart to be pure and totally acceptable to God. I call my heart out of the ghetto of sin and to be located into the palace of righteousness and holiness.

By the power of God, I declare that my heart shall not be a dumping ground for greed, graft, godlessness or any form of orgy in Jesus' name.

Every form of heart association with haters of God in my life are hereby terminated in Jesus' name. My heart is separated from evil covenant or ties in Jesus' name. Out of my heart shall proceed good thoughts. I declare that I will only think about what is true, honourable, right, and pure in Jesus' name. My heart shall be a garden where lovely, admirable, excellent and praiseworthy things will grow and flourish in Jesus' name.

I am strong and stable and not feeble and shaky in my heart in Jesus' name. In times of challenges and difficulties I shall remain strong and not shifty in Jesus' name. Out of my heart shall proceed life changing virtue that will shape my world and the world around me for good in Jesus' name.

Whatever I Touch Shall Prosper

Isaiah 53:10 – *Yet it pleased the LORD to bruise Him; He has put Him to grief. When You make His soul an offering for sin, He shall see His seed, He shall prolong His days, And the pleasure of the LORD shall prosper in His hand.*

DECLARATION: With my hands I shall do great exploits in Jesus' name. My hands shall not be dipped into iniquity neither shall they drip with sin, but shall be fully dedicated to Jehovah God in Jesus' name.

I command every evil hand raised against me to dry up and wither away in Jesus' name. All hands struck together in threat against me shall not complete what they set out to do in Jesus' name.

By the power in the name of Jesus, my hands shall be strong to carry out good works for my Master. Whatever I purpose to do for the advancement of my Father's Kingdom and for my wellbeing, my hands shall carry out in Jesus' name. I declare that my Father shall strengthen my hands for great work and mighty deeds in Jesus' name.

All evil schemes planned to weaken my hands shall utterly fail and they shall come to nothing. Those who sit to plan my destruction and stand to distract me from my life assignment shall be made into nothing in Jesus' name. My path and purpose shall get stronger and stronger, while the plan and purpose of the enemies of my life shall get weaker in Jesus' name.

By the mark of the blood of Jesus, I decree that whatever my hands touch shall prosper. Through my hands healing shall flow forth. Dead and dying souls, physical bodies, businesses, and relationships shall come back to life at the touch of my hands. When I lay my hands on the sick, they shall recover in Jesus' name.

I Shall Step into My High Places

Habakkuk 3:19 – *The LORD God is my strength; He will make my* *feet like deer's feet, And He will make me walk on my high hills.*

DECLARATION: With my feet I shall climb to higher grounds in Jesus' name. I shall stand firm and shall not wobble or stumble because my Father shall steady my feet. My feet shall not walk the walk of shame, neither shall they be quick to walk into sin in Jesus' name.

By the power of the word of God, my feet shall be guided in the right direction and my path shall be lighted in Jesus' name. I shall never walk in darkness neither shall I stray away in confusion.

My path shall not cross with disaster and my way will be divergent from destruction in Jesus' name.

I command you my feet to be directed in the way of prosperity and piety. The great power of God shall order my feet in the path of life in Jesus' name.

My feet shall be called beautiful because it will proclaim the good news in Jesus' name. My feet shall take every step for Jesus and shall take no step for the devil. My feet shall only run errands for the King of kings in Jesus' name.

CHAPTER TEN

I AM SPECIAL AND NOT COMMON

Like A Lion

Genesis 49:8-10

8 "Judah, your brothers will praise you. You will grasp your enemies by the neck. All your relatives will bow before you.

9 Judah, my son, is a young lion that has finished eating its prey. Like a lion he crouches and lies down; like a lioness—who dares to rouse him?

10 The sceptre will not depart from Judah, nor the ruler's staff from his descendants, until the coming of the one to whom it belongs, the one whom all nations will honour."

DECLARATION: I am of the lineage of Jesus – the lion of the tribe of Judah, and like a lion, I exercise my authority and power over my enemies. I shall dominate and not be dominated in Jesus' name. I shall dominate situations and circumstances in Jesus' name.

The roar of the word of God in my mouth shall put the enemy to flight in Jesus' name. Wherever they resist me the strength of my hands shall subdue them.

Like a lion, I am strong, I am bold and I shall not be denied my portion in Jesus' name.

Like a lion, I shall be revered and honoured in my allocated territory in Jesus' name.

Like a lion, I shall rule and reign in my allotted territory. Circumstances and life situations shall bow to me. At my roar of prayer, strangers and upstarts shall flee in Jesus' name.

Like an Eagle

Exodus 19:4 – 'You have seen what I did to the Egyptians, and how I bore you on eagles' wings and brought you to Myself."

Deuteronomy 14:12 – But these you shall not eat: the eagle, the vulture, the buzzard...

Leviticus 11:13 – And these you shall regard as an abomination among the birds; they shall not be eaten, they are an abomination: the eagle, the vulture, the buzzard...

Isaiah 40:31 – *But those who wait on the LORD Shall renew their strength; They shall mount up with wings like eagles, They shall run and not be weary, They shall walk and not faint.*

Psalm 103:5 – *Who satisfies your mouth with good things, So that your youth is renewed like the eagle's.*

Proverbs 13:18-19 – *There are three things which are too wonderful for me, Yes, four which I do not understand: The way of an eagle in the air, The way of a serpent on a rock, The way of a ship in the midst of the sea, And the way of a man with a virgin.*

DECLARATION: I declare in the name of Jesus that like an eagle I shall not be meat or prey for anyone. Abomination! – Let no one lay their teeth on me.

Like an eagle, I declare that my youth shall be renewed in Jesus' name. By the great power of God I shall say in my old age – "as my strength was 40 years ago, so my strength is now." Like an eagle, I shall shed old cover for new one in Jesus' name. Old anointing will give way for new in the name of Jesus. As I increase in age, my physical strength shall not abate neither will my vision dim in Jesus' name. The God of Moses shall be my God, the God of Caleb shall be my God, the Strength of Israel shall be my God in Jesus' name.

Like an eagle, I shall be an absolute mystery to my enemies. The source of my strength, and the fountain of my success shall never be discovered by those who seek to do me harm. Like an eagle, I shall be a wonder to my friends. Many shall admire me and seek to follow me as I follow Jesus. Like an eagle, I shall be a beauty to behold, and a joy to those who see me soar in Jesus' name. Like an eagle, I shall fly high and go far. My progress and reach shall not be curtailed or limited in Jesus' name. I will not live or operate from low, but from high places. By my spiritual nature, I declare that I am an HIGH FLYER in Jesus' name. Like an eagle, my eyes are sharp to see far, the focus is strong and trained, and my determination is unwavering in Jesus' name. Whatever the Lord has provided for me to eat, I shall not miss it in Jesus' name.

Like an eagle, I receive the wisdom to raise generations of eagles. My children (biological and spiritual), like eaglets shall inherit the nature of God in me. From my generation to generation, only eagles shall come out of my household. I shall not bear chickens, I shall not raise chickens or ducks but eagles and eagles only in the name of Jesus.

My Heavenly Father, who carried me out of Egypt shall keep bearing me on His wings. I am carried in Jesus' name. Amen.

CHAPTER ELEVEN

MY SPIRITUAL POSTURE

Psalm 1:1–3

[1] *Blessed is the man Who walks not in the counsel of the ungodly, Nor stands in the path of sinners, Nor sits in the seat of the scornful;*

[2] *But his delight is in the law of the LORD, And in His law he meditates day and night.*

[3] *He shall be like a tree Planted by the rivers of water, That brings forth its fruit in its season, Whose leaf also shall not wither; And whatever he does shall prosper.*

Sitting

DECLARATION: I declare in the name of Jesus that I shall not sit in the seat of shame and ignominy. My seat is with the righteous and beloved of God. I shall sit and remain in the place of honour that the Lord has prepared for me in Jesus' name. My seat is secure and shall not be taken away from me. In my family, my seat is secure; in my work place, my place is well secure; in my service to God and to humanity, my seat is secure in Jesus' name.

I declare in the name of Jesus that I shall not be uprooted or upended, neither shall I be overturned from the place of blessing the Lord has established for me.

I am secure, settled and firmly rooted in God's blessings in Jesus' name.

I rise up now from that seat that is not meant for me. I command everyone and anyone sitting on the seat the Lord has reserved for me to get up now in Jesus' name. I take my place now, and I settle in my allotted seat in the name of Jesus.

I declare boldly according to scripture that "I am seated in heavenly places with Christ Jesus my Lord". I am above and not beneath, I am in Christ and therefore I am not exposed.

My seat is with the mighty, the princes and the rulers.

I am a prince on horse back and I shall not swap my position with servants who walk on foot. (Ecclesiastes 10:7).

Standing

DECLARATION: I declare in the name of Jesus that I shall stand tall and not crouch to beg or to be stamped upon in the name of Jesus. My path will not cross with those of sinners, neither will I seek out the way of transgressors to stand with them. I shall only be found standing in the congregation of the righteous.

By the power in the name of Jesus, I shall stand up against every plot and agenda of the evil one. No running or turning for me in the name of Jesus. When the enemy comes against me in one way, he will run away in seven ways.

As the Lord God my Redeemers lives, I declare again that the enemy shall turn his back and flee as soon as he sees me in Jesus' name. All those who are incensed against me shall never see my back, neither shall I ever bow before my adversary in Jesus' name. I declare again that I shall stand tall and tower over every opposition of the enemy in the name of Jesus.

My standing in the Kingdom of my God shall not be compromised, neither shall my place of honour in the church of Christ be taken away from me in Jesus' name. I am a blessing to my generation, because I shall stand to be counted. I pledge in the name of Jesus that by the help of the Holy Spirit of God

I shall stand up for Whom I believe in, and for what I believe.

Fear will not make me crawl or slither away in the face of opposition. The One in me cannot bow to anyone neither will I bow the bow of defeat to any temporal power or evil celestial power. I bow in total submission only to my God and King. I am standing in Christ Jesus. I shall not fall neither shall I be brought to my knees in Jesus' name.

I am victorious through Him who redeemed me. Amen.

Walking

DECLARATION: By the power in the name of Jesus, I boldly declare that I shall not walk the walk of shame.

From now on, I shall never walk alone, because the Lord is with me. The angels of the Lord shall encamp around wherever I go in Jesus' name. To my front, back, above and beneath me, I am surrounded by the mercy of God. Goodness and mercy shall follow me wherever I go in Jesus' name. My feet shall not saunter into trouble, neither will my legs stray into terror in Jesus' name.

Every step I take and every stride I make, shall be for the advancement of the Kingdom of my King. I purpose in my heart that I shall walk to the farthest end of the earth in obedience to my God in Jesus' name.

I declare and pronounce clearly that by the mercies of the Lord, I shall be in good health all my days in Jesus' name. As Moses' strength did not abate in his old age, I declare in Jesus' name that no one will carry me around in my old age, but with my two feet I will walk until the Lord returns or comes to take me home.

The jingle of blessing and the sound of glory shall go forth from me as I walk through life in Jesus' name. By the anointing of the Holy Spirit, I declare that I shall leave a trail of sweet aroma of God's glory and beauty as I make my way through life in Jesus' name.

Above all, I declare that I shall walk in the spirit and not in the flesh. I shall be a joy to behold and a pleasure to the eyes as I walk through life victorious in Jesus' name.

Flying (Soaring)

DECLARARTION: By the great mercy of God, I declare that I shall soar with wings like an eagle. I confess that I am a high flyer and not a worm crawling through life in Jesus' name. The wind of the Holy Spirit under my wings shall carry me every moment of my life in Jesus' name. My ascendancy to the top shall not be by the flapping of the wings but by the strong wind of God in Jesus' name. Effortlessly, I shall rise to the very top in Jesus' name. My wings shall be strong and its span shall be long in Jesus' name. I receive the power and capacity to carry those coming after me unto great heights in Jesus' name.

I will not attain great heights alone. As the Lord raises me, I will be a blessing to many others who will rise with me. I declare that that I shall not fall nor crash as I climb in Jesus' name. The hand of God that holds me is strong enough to keep me to the end in Jesus' name.

CHAPTER TWELVE

THE ELEMENTS SHALL WORK FOR ME

Sun

Proverbs 4:18 – *But the path of the just is like the shining sun, That shines ever brighter unto the perfect day.*

Psalm 84:10-11

¹⁰ *For a day in Your courts is better than a thousand. I would rather be a doorkeeper in the house of my God Than dwell in the tents of wickedness.*

¹¹ *For the LORD God is a sun and shield; The LORD will give grace and glory; No good thing will He withhold From those who walk uprightly.*

CONFESSION: I confess in the name of Jesus that by the shining of the Light of God on my life, I shall enjoy grace and full glory.

Because the light of God is over me nothing good shall be withheld from me in Jesus' name. By the grace of God I shall walk uprightly, and live uprightly in Jesus' name.

Psalm 121:5-6 *The LORD is your keeper; The LORD is your shade at your right hand.*
The sun shall not strike you by day, Nor the moon by night. (Sun not work against me)

DECLARATION: The brightness of my sun shall not work against me but in my favour. My success shall not burn me, neither will my victory be my undoing in Jesus' name.

Isaiah 60: 20 – *Your sun shall no longer go down, Nor shall your moon withdraw itself; For the LORD will be your everlasting light, And the days of your mourning shall be ended.*

Isaiah 30: 26 – *Moreover the light of the moon will be as the light of the sun, And the light of the sun will be sevenfold, As the light of seven days, In the day that the LORD binds up the bruise of His people And heals the stroke of their wound.*

Malachi 4: 2 – *"But to you who fear My name The Sun of Righteousness shall arise With healing in His wings; And you shall go out And grow fat like stall-fed calves."*

DECLARATION: I declare in the name of Jesus that my sun shall not set in its prime. My life like the noonday sun shall shine brighter and brighter in Jesus' name. My success is long term and not short term, my victory is eternal and not (ephemeral) temporary.

CONFESSION: I confess in the name of Jesus that by the shining of the Light of God on my life, I shall enjoy grace and full glory.

Because the light of God is over me nothing good shall be withheld from me in Jesus' name. By the grace of God I shall walk uprightly, and live uprightly in Jesus' name.

The brightness of my sun shall not work against me but in my favour. My success shall not burn me, neither will my victory be my undoing in Jesus' name.

I declare and cry to my Father – My sun shall not go down in Jesus' name!!! The intensity of the brightness of my life's sun shall increase daily. I shall not go into obscurity nor be brought into ignominy. In the kingdom of my God, I shall remain a bright light all my days in Jesus' name.

Sun of Righteousness arise on me in Jesus' name.

Because we are the light of this city, nation and the world, we hereby command darkness of sin, sickness and economic woes to disappear now in Jesus' name. Our light is shining in the darkness, and the darkness cannot and shall not overcome it in Jesus' name. Amen.

Rain

Ezekiel 34:26 – *I will make them and the places all around My hill a blessing; and I will cause showers to come down in their season; there shall be showers of blessing.*

DECLARATION: I declare that the rain of God's blessings shall fall over our lives in Jesus' name.

Every dry patch in my life shall be soaked with God's shower of blessing in Jesus' name. (Shower of Joy, peace)

I command every righteous seed I have sown to gather into a cloud—and let my cloud yield abundant rain in Jesus' name.

The cloud of God's blessing over my life shall not disperse but shall fall to my ground in Jesus' name.

Because my heaven shall open, I shall never experience spiritual drought again in Jesus' name.

Because my heaven shall be open, I shall never experience financial drought again in Jesus' name.

Because my heaven shall open and pour down rain, I shall never experience any form of drought ever again in Jesus' name.

As my rain falls, my ground shall yield a bountiful harvest in Jesus' name.

From now on, my rain shall fall in its due season in Jesus' name.

FATHER, I PRAISE YOU!
THANK YOU FOR ANSWERING MY PRAYERS!

PERSONAL NOTES

PERSONAL NOTES

_____

_____

_____

_____

_____

_____

_____

_____

_____

_____

PERSONAL NOTES

_____

_____

_____

_____

_____

_____

_____

_____

_____

_____

_____

PERSONAL NOTES

_____

_____

_____

_____

_____

_____

_____

_____

_____

_____

_____

PERSONAL NOTES

PERSONAL NOTES

_____

_____

_____

_____

_____

_____

_____

_____

_____

_____